AlphaTales Teaching Guide

Lessons, ABC Activities, & Reproducible
Mini-Book Versions of All 26 Storybooks

SCHOLASTIC
PROFESSIONAL BOOKS

New York • Toronto • London • Auckland • Sydney • New Delhi • Mexico City • Hong Kong

Acknowledgements: Thanks to Joan Novelli and Wiley Blevins for contributing teaching tips and activities. Some of the activities in this book are adapted from *Phonics from A to Z* by Wiley Blevins (Scholastic Professional Books, 1998).

Cover and interior design by Norma Ortiz

ISBN-13: 978-0-439-16523-5
ISBN-10: 0-439-16523-7

Table of Contents

Teaching with AlphaTales

The Mini-Books

A Note to Teachers

Learning the alphabet and the sounds that letters represent both individually and in combination with other letters is essential to learning to read.

Two powerful predictors of early reading success are alphabet recognition (knowing the names of the letters and the sounds they represent) and phonemic awareness (understanding that a word is made up of a series of discrete sounds). These two skills open the gate to early reading. Without a thorough knowledge of letters and an understanding that words are made up of sounds, children cannot learn to read. The *AlphaTales* series is designed to help you help your students develop these important skills.

Throughout a child's preschool years, letters are learned by singing the rhythmic ABC song, being exposed to alphabet books, watching educational programs and videos, and having family members point out and identify letters in environmental print and in the child's name. Children eagerly engage in these activities—all with the understanding that this small set of somewhat strange markings holds the key to unlocking our written language.

Because of this early exposure to the alphabet, many children enter school already able to recognize a few printed letters and to say their ABC's. However, being able to say the names of the letters is not the same as "knowing" the letters. In order to learn to read, children must be able to identify the printed forms of all the letters in and out of sequence and learn the most frequent sound that is attached to each letter.

But it is not just recognizing letters—both upper and lowercase, in and out of sequence—that is critical. It is the speed, or automaticity, with which children recognize the letters that is important. For automaticity to take place, children actually need to over-learn the letters of the alphabet. Research shows that students who can recognize letters with accuracy and speed have an easier time learning the sounds associated with the letters than those children who are struggling with alphabet recognition.

The *AlphaTales* series can be an effective tool in helping you teach all of these crucial aspects of alphabet recognition. The stories will enable you to:

◆ help children learn letter sequence.

◆ help children associate a letter with a sound.

◆ help build children's phonemic awareness skills.

◆ support beginning readers' oral language development.

◆ help children build vocabulary and word knowledge.

Of course, a variety of alphabet books are important in any early childhood classroom. But while most alphabet books allow a page or two for each letter, the *AlphaTales* series devotes an entire book to each letter, enabling you to immerse students in language that targets the letter you are studying. In fact, research shows that as children learn letters, they frequently become interested in learning more about them—their sounds and how to use them to write words. The *AlphaTales* stories offer a language-rich context for these explorations.

Teaching the most common one-to-one correspondence of letter to sound helps children develop and understand the alphabetic principle. For some children, this is a tremendous "Aha!" Reading becomes a kind of puzzle in which children map a sound onto a letter or letter cluster and blend the sounds together to read words. For some children, the process requires more practice and time. These children need additional opportunities to hear the sounds, play with sounds and letters, write letters, and practice reading simple words using sounds and letters they have learned.

The instruction that accompanies the *AlphaTales* series is tailored to help you maximize the benefits of each book in the program. This instruction focuses on teaching children to distinguish sounds, letters, and words. Some additional suggestions for instruction include the following:

◆ As soon as possible, build words using the letter-sound correspondences children learn.

◆ Engage children's multiple senses—have them say, touch, write, and feel the alphabet in many ways.

◆ Note letters in the child's environment. Create an interest in and excitement about letters and words.

◆ As soon as possible, help children use letters in writing. If a child cannot spell complete words, have the child write parts of words in lists or stories you are writing.

◆ During handwriting instruction, always have children say the sound a letter stands for when they are practicing writing the letter.

◆ Read lots of ABC books and have children make their own alphabet books.

Remember, a child's long educational journey often begins with a simple tune—"A, B, C, D, E, F, G. . . Now I know my ABC's. Tell me what you think of me." Since English is an alphabetic language, it makes sense to start children at a young age learning this series of squiggles and lines that, when combined, create something spectacular—printed words. As you use the *AlphaTales* series to teach children the letters of the alphabet and their corresponding sounds, always enjoy the books with them. Share your excitement and interest in our sometimes complex, yet always fascinating, written language. Introducing children to the joys of reading is one of the most important things you can do!

Wiley Blevins
Ed.M. Harvard University

Welcome to AlphaTales

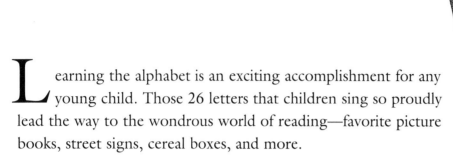

Learning the alphabet is an exciting accomplishment for any young child. Those 26 letters that children sing so proudly lead the way to the wondrous world of reading—favorite picture books, street signs, cereal boxes, and more.

AlphaTales offer a fun and easy way to capitalize on children's natural interest in learning the alphabet. Each simple, imaginative story introduces children to an animal "mascot" whose name begins with a letter of the alphabet. Students will meet the doughnut-loving Detective Dog, a nice young newt named Nate, and Zack, a zebra with no zip—along with many others. Each animal mascot will lead children on an exploration of that letter through an engaging story.

Other features in the *AlphaTales* program are:

◆ an alphabet activity at the end of each story that invites children to find objects in an illustrated scene that begin with the featured letter (see pages 14–15 of picture books)

◆ an easy-to-learn rhyming cheer designed to help children remember key words that begin with the target letter as well as to celebrate learning (see page 16 of picture books)

◆ teaching notes and activity suggestions to help you introduce the *AlphaTales*, build on each story's alphabet lesson, strengthen students' reading skills, and assess students' progress (see pages 9–17 of this teacher book)

◆ reproducible patterns for making mini-book versions of all 26 stories in the *AlphaTales* series to give students further exposure to and practice with each letter (see pages 21–124 of this teacher book).

Teaching Tips

Keep these tips in mind as you introduce and share *AlphaTales* books with your students.

Choosing Letter Sequence

There is no one correct order in which to teach the letter names. Because many children come to school knowing the traditional ABC song, you may opt to cover the letters of the alphabet in the same order. Some teachers prefer to first teach the letters in children's names, since these letters have special meaning to them.

Reading specialist Wiley Blevins recommends the following guidelines in teaching children the alphabet, regardless of the sequence you choose:

◆ Decide whether it is appropriate to teach the uppercase and lowercase letters together or separately, depending on your students' age and ability level. Preschoolers should be taught uppercase letters first, whereas K–1 students should be taught lowercase first since they encounter these letter forms more often in print. If children already have a good deal of alphabet knowledge, it may be appropriate to teach both cases together.

◆ Teach children the names of letters first, since most letter names are closely related to their sounds (the exceptions are *h, q, w, y, g,* and the short vowels). This will help children understand the "alphabetic principle": Each letter stands for a sound.

◆ Once children know the names of letters, teach their shapes and the most common sound associated with each one. Connecting a key word and picture with each letter is an ideal way to grasp the letter-sound relationship. As children write a letter, be sure to have them say its name and the sound associated with it to reinforce this connection.

◆ Help children see the similarities and differences among letters. For example, the letters *b* and *d* are similar in appearance, but the small circles on each face different directions. Recognizing these subtle differences is essential in learning to identify letters of the alphabet when they are out of sequence. On the following page you'll find a table that includes pairs of letters that children sometimes confuse because they are similar in appearance.

Confusable Letter Pairs

Lowercase				Uppercase	
a-d	c-o	h-n	n-u	C-G	M-N
a-o	d-q	h-u	p-q	D-O	M-W
b-d	d-g	i-j	u-v	E-F	O-Q
b-h	d-p	i-l	v-w	I-J	P-R
b-p	f-t	k-y	v-y	I-L	U-V
b-q	g-p	m-n		K-X	V-Y
c-e	g-q	m-w		L-T	

◆ Avoid teaching the following letter groups at the same time, since research shows they are particularly confusing for students:

- e, a, s, c, o
- b, d, p, o, g, h
- f, l, t, k, i, h
- n, m, u, h, r

2 Before Reading

Introduce the featured letter of the *AlphaTales* book you are reading with an assortment of quick activities. Repetition helps teach recognition. Variety helps meet each learner's needs.

◆ Use a wet sponge to write the featured letter on the chalkboard. Can children guess the letter before it disappears?

◆ Write the letter, uppercase and lowercase, on chart paper. Trace the letter formation as children do the same in the air, on their desks, in their palms, or each other's backs.

◆ Help children see how the featured letter is like other letters they know. For example, they might recognize that *a* has a circle like *g*, *b*, and *d*.

◆ Ask children if they know what sound the letter makes. Let them take turns naming words they know that start with this sound.

◆ Introduce the main character of the story. Ask students if they can guess why the author picked this animal and name. (Each begins with the featured letter.)

◆ Hold up the cover of the book. Read the title aloud and ask children to look closely at the illustration. What do they think the story will be about? Flip the book over and read the story summary on the back cover. Were students' predictions correct?

⭐3 During Reading

The first time through, just read the selected *AlphaTales* book aloud. This will allow children to enjoy the story and get a feel for the language. Get more out of the story with these tips.

◆ Reread the story, this time asking children to look and listen for the featured letter. Let children signal you when they hear the letter at the beginning of a word—for example, by holding up cards on which they've written the letter.

◆ On another reading of the story, ask children to closely examine the illustration on each page. Do they see anything pictured that begins with the letter you are studying? Can they find the word for this object in the text?

◆ After several readings, encourage children to chime in on predictable words. They'll delight in seeing how many words they know!

⭐4 After Reading

Extend the learning with activities that build on each *AlphaTales* story.

◆ Share the two-page illustration at the end of each *AlphaTales* book. Challenge children to find objects in the picture that start with the featured letter. On the inside back cover of each book, you'll find a list of objects included in each activity spread. Be aware that these lists include only nouns. Children may actually come up with more words than appear on the lists; for example, they may name adjectives (such as *yellow* in the activity spread for the "Y" book) or verbs (such as *jump* in the activity spread for the "J" book). They also may pick up on subtle visual details that are not included in the answer lists (for example, the characters' body parts such as *nose* in the "N" book or *elbow* in the "E" book). Be open to all student responses.

◆ Have fun with the cheer that accompanies each *AlphaTales* book. After practicing the original cheer, let students make a new cheer. Write the cheer on chart paper, leaving blanks for each word that starts with the featured letter. Have children take turns filling in the blanks to complete the cheer. Make mini-megaphones out of rolled up paper. Shout it out!

◆ Play a quick game to reinforce the target letter's sound. For example, if you're teaching the letter *s*, say the sound for *s* and then say a word that starts with *s*, stretching out or repeating the initial sound—for example, *ssssseal*. Let children take turns saying other words that start with that sound, also stretching out the beginning—for example, *sssssilly* and *SSSSSSunday*.

5 Using the Mini-Books

The reproducible mini-books are an excellent way to strengthen students' skills and build a home-school connection. Here are some ideas for using the mini-books both in and out of the classroom.

◆ After you've read an *AlphaTales* story aloud several times, provide children with the reproducible mini-book pattern and help them make their very own copy of the story. Students can then follow along in their mini-books as you read the story again. Model reading strategies along the way—for example, each story provides plenty of opportunities to work with initial letter-sound relationships.

◆ Make audio recordings of the stories and put them in a special listening center. Provide copies of the mini-books so that students can follow along with the tapes.

To Make the Mini-Books

1. Make double sided copies of the mini-book pages. (You should have two double-side copies for each one.)

2. Cut the pages in half along the dashed line.

3. Position the pages so that the lettered spreads (A, B, C, D) are face up. Place the B spread on top of the A spread. Then, place the C and D spread on top of those in sequence.

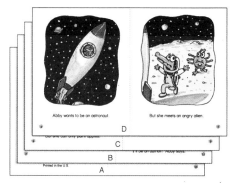

4. Fold the pages in half along the solid line. Make sure all the pages are in the proper order. Staple them together along the book's spine.

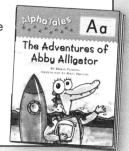

◆ As you teach each letter of the alphabet, create a mini learning center where students can gain additional practice recognizing and writing the letter. The mini-books can form the basis of one learning center activity. Simply place copies of the mini-book in the center, and have children circle all the words they can find in the story that begin with the target letter.

◆ Ask each child to bring in a shoe box from home. Then set out a variety of art materials and allow students to decorate the boxes (preferably with alphabet motifs!). Children can use the boxes to house their very own *AlphaTales* mini-book library. Students will enjoy returning to the stories again and again.

◆ Let children take home their mini-books to read with family members. Children can "announce" the letter of the alphabet your class is currently studying by wearing a special badge. The badge can also serve as an invitation to parents and caregivers to read the latest *AlphaTales* story with their child. Children and adults can then look around their home (on food labels, the mail, catalogs, and so on) for more words that begin with the target letter.

Making the Badge

Photocopy the pattern for each student. Trim the badge to size, and help children fill in the letter of the day and title of the latest *AlphaTales* book. Children can then color the badge. Punch a hole at the top and string with yarn so children can wear the badge around their neck.

This week we're studying the letter _____

Let's read

_____

together.

⑥ Assessment

The following suggestions will help you assess students' alphabet recognition skills. There are several critical components of alphabet recognition that students need to master in order to lay the foundation for future reading success:

◆ Does the child know the letter's name?

◆ Does he or she know the sound the letter makes?

◆ Can he or she recognize the letter both in and out of sequence, in both its upper– and lowercase form?

◆ Can the child write the letter, both upper– and lowercase, independently— that is, without copying or tracing it?

◆ What is the degree of automaticity, or speed, with which the child can accomplish these tasks?

On page 15 of this book, you'll find a reproducible you can use to help gauge students' skill level.

◆ Depending on how much prior alphabet knowledge children bring to the classroom, they may need different amounts of time to develop letter recognition skills. For students who are struggling, provide additional time to practice identifying and writing the letters and to explore letter-sound relationships. Be sure to engage all of children's senses, and tailor activities to students' different learning styles. For example, you might plan a kinesthetic alphabet activity in which students connect—and demonstrate—an action word with each letter of the alphabet: *D* is for dance; *J* is for jump; *R* is for run; and so on. For a tactile experience, children can form letter shapes using clay. For visually oriented learners, paste pictures of objects that begin with each letter of the alphabet on 26 separate 4" x 5" index cards. Write the letters of the alphabet on 26 other cards. Small groups of children will enjoy matching picture and letter cards in a game of alphabet lotto.

◆ Memory devices are a useful way to help children who are having difficulty distinguishing between letters that are similar in appearance. For example, if you find a child tends to confuse lowercase *h* with lowercase *n*, point out that lowercase *h* looks like it's raising its "hand" (an "h" word). Simple rhymes also make effective pneumonic devices; for example:
    "Big M, little m—let's stand them on their head.
     Now the M's are gone and we have W's instead!"

Name _____ Date _____

Alphabet Recognition Assessment

Have the student draw a line to match each uppercase letter with its lowercase form. Ask student to name each letter as he or she makes a match. Circle the letters whose names the child correctly identifies.

Upper/lowercase Match

A	c	B	d	H	h	P	r	K	o	M	x
C	v	D	f	I	l	Q	z	O	k	N	y
G	a	E	e	J	i	R	q	S	t	W	w
V	u	F	b	L	j	Z	p	T	s	X	n
U	g									Y	m

To assess the student's ability to recognize letters out of sequence, ask him or her to point to each letter on the chart below and say its name. Circle the letters that the child correctly identifies.

Upper/lowercase Random Order Mix

E	B	o	h	P	f	N	x	I
a	q	G	m	R	L	j	v	k
U	c	Z	W	d	T	y	s	

Quick-and-Easy Activities

You can use the following activities with any of the *AlphaTales* books to strengthen literacy skills in meaningful and memorable ways.

AlphaTales Around the Room

This charming alphabet frieze will reinforce letter recognition skills and give children a resource they'll enjoy using again and again as they learn to recognize and form letters.

◆ Write the letters of the alphabet on slips of paper and place them in a bag.

◆ Have each child select a letter at random. Record children's letters on a class list and place with your *AlphaTales* materials.

◆ Each time you read an *AlphaTales* book, have the child who selected that letter make a piece of an alphabet frieze. Have this child write the letter on a sheet of good-quality drawing paper (use the same size for each letter), draw a picture of the main character, and write the character's name. Display on the wall at children's eye level. Add to the frieze with each book you read.

Tongue-Twister Fun

Students will quickly notice the alliterative language in each of the *AlphaTales* stories. Reread a sentence from the story you are using, and ask students what sound they hear repeated at the beginning of some of the words. Write the sentence on the board and invite a volunteer to underline the beginning letters that are the same. Share a familiar tongue twister to reinforce the concept of alliteration: *Sally sells seashells at the seashore.* Challenge children to create their own tongue twisters based on the main characters in the books. For example, after sharing *Rosie Rabbit's Radish,*

have students make up tongue twisters about Rosie Rabbit to reinforce the letter *R*. You might write down their tongue twisters for each letter and put them together to make a book. Or record them on an audiotape for listening fun.

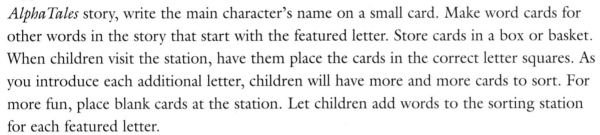

Alpha Sorting Station

This sorting station will reinforce letter recognition and initial letter sounds for each letter you teach. Set up the sorting station by dividing tagboard into 26 squares. Write one letter of the alphabet (upper– and lowercase) in each square. As you introduce each new *AlphaTales* story, write the main character's name on a small card. Make word cards for other words in the story that start with the featured letter. Store cards in a box or basket. When children visit the station, have them place the cards in the correct letter squares. As you introduce each additional letter, children will have more and more cards to sort. For more fun, place blank cards at the station. Let children add words to the sorting station for each featured letter.

AlphaTales Word Wall

Use your *AlphaTales* stories to build an interactive word wall that supports students in letter recognition, letter-sound relationships, and more.

◆ Start by writing upper– and lowercase letters on a large sheet of craft paper. Leave plenty of space between letters so that children have room to add pictures and words.

◆ Beginning with the first letter you teach, say the letter aloud and trace both the upper– and lowercase forms on the word wall as children do the same in the air or on their desks.

◆ After sharing the story once, reread it, asking children to listen for the words that start with the featured letter. Write the words on the word wall and draw pictures to go with them.

◆ Let children add to the word wall on their own, using the books to help spell words or asking one another for help. Revisit the word wall often to read new words.

I Spy AlphaTales

Let students make "I Spy" pictures to go with *AlphaTales* stories. Have them place the main character in a new scene, surrounded by things that start with the featured letter. Before they begin working, block off a strip at the bottom of students' papers to leave room for a sentence. Let children dictate sentences about their pictures. For example, "I spy an alligator, apple pie, ant, anteater, angelfish, accordion, automobile, artwork, …." Display children's "I Spy" pictures. Can they find all the items in one another's pictures?

Mini-Books

Aa Cheer

A is for alligator and acorns on trees

A is for "Ah-choo!" when you sneeze

A is for apples baked in a pie

A is for airplane up in the sky

Hooray for **A**, big and small—

the most awesome, amazing letter of all!

The Adventures of Abby Alligator

By Maria Fleming
Illustrated by Matt Phillips

Abby Alligator writes all about her adventures as an acrobat, an artist, an animal doctor, an astronaut, and an actor.

Abby Alligator is ready to work.
What will Abby do?

For Jess B.,
in honor of her own AMAZING adventures
in the world of work.

🐾 🐾 🐾 🐾

A

Being an author is AWESOME!

13

Abby wants to be an acrobat.

Then Abby has an AMAZING idea.
"I'll be an author!" Abby says.

2

B

11

Abby can't think of any other jobs.

But she's afraid of falling.

Uh-oh. I forgot my lines again.

Abby wants to be an actor.

AHCHOO

Abby wants to be an animal doctor.
But she's allergic to aardvarks.

Abby wants to be an artist.
But she can only paint apples.

But she is awful.

Abby wants to be an astronaut.

But she meets an angry alien.

Bb Cheer

B is for bear, bubbles, and boat

B is for buttons on your coat

B is for bicycle, bunny, and bat

B is for bee—imagine that!

Hooray for **B**, big and small—

The best, most beautiful letter of all!

Bb

Bubble Bear

BY MAXWELL HIGGINS
ILLUSTRATED BY MAXIE CHAMBLISS

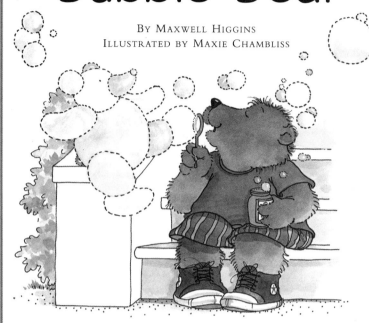

So Bear showed Badger how to blow big bubbles and itsy-bitsy bubbles. He showed her how to blow a bubble beard, a bubble bell, and a bubble birthday cake.

Bear was the best bubble blower on his block. Bear could blow great big bubbles.

A

He showed her how to blow a bubble bunny, a bubble bear, and a bubble badger. And Bear even showed Badger how to blow a great big bubble beast!

13

Bear could blow itsy-bitsy bubbles.

"Bear, I am sorry I called you a baby," said Badger. "Will you show me how you blow such beautiful bubbles?"

2

B

11

"Only babies are afraid of bubbles!"
Bear told Badger.

Bear could even blow a bubble beard!

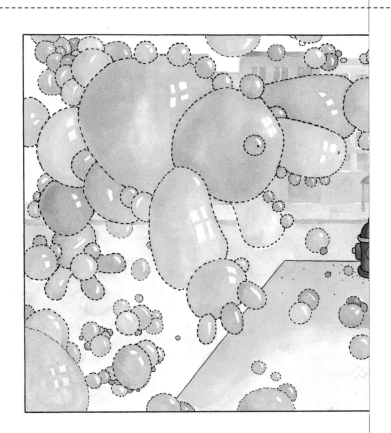

...a great big bubble beast!

and a bubble bunny

and, of course, a bubble bear!

Bear could blow lots of bubble shapes, too.

Bear could blow a bubble bell

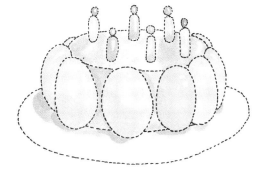

and a bubble birthday cake

"Ahhhhh!" yelled Badger.
She ran behind a bush.

One day, Badger saw Bear blowing bubbles.
Badger was a bully.
Everyone on the block was afraid of her.

"Only babies blow bubbles," Badger told Bear.
But Bear kept right on blowing.
He blew and blew until he had blown...

Cc Cheer

C is for cat, **C** is for cap

C is for carrot, crayon, and clap

C is for camel, cow, cup, and car

C is for cookies in a cookie jar

Hooray for **C**, big and small—

the coolest, craziest letter of all!

Copycats

BY MARIA FLEMING
ILLUSTRATED BY HANS WILHELM

Clyde crashes into Cleo.
The cups crash to the ground.

Clyde and Cleo are cats—copycats!
"I bet you can't do what I can do,"
says Clyde.
"I can too!" says Cleo.

For Catie —
a Cutie with a capital C

❧ ❧ ❧ ❧

A

Clyde looks at Cleo. Cleo looks at Clyde.
They are both covered in cocoa.
"I can stop being a copycat,"
says Clyde. "Can you?"
"I can too," says Cleo.

13

"I can do a cartwheel," says Clyde.
"Can you?"
"I can too!" says Cleo.

2

B

"I can too!" says Clyde.
"Look out for the car!" yells Cleo.

11

"I can carry a cup of cocoa on my head,"
says Cleo. "Can you?"

"I can ride a camel," says Cleo.
"Can you?"
"I can too!" says Clyde.

"I can grow carrots, corn, and cabbages,"
says Clyde. "Can you?"

"I can too!" says Cleo.

"I can bake a coconut cake,"
says Clyde. "Can you?"

C

"I can too!" says Cleo.

"I can build a castle," says Cleo.
"Can you?"

D

"I can too!" says Clyde.

Dd Cheer

D is for dog and doughnut, too

D is for dolphin in the ocean blue

D is for doll, doctor, and door

D is for duck and dinosaur

Hooray for **D**, big and small—

the most dazzling, delightful letter of all!

14

Detective Dog and the Disappearing Doughnuts

BY VALERIE GARFIELD
ILLUSTRATED BY PAUL HARVEY

Dave told Detective Dog that he only
pretended the doughnuts had disappeared.
Dave made the trail of doughnut dust
to lead the detective to the party.

12

Detective Dog went to Dave's Diner
every day for dinner.

1

For Jordan,
who is letter perfect
(and who loves a good doughnut).

Detective Dog was delighted with the party.
There were dazzling decorations and dandy gifts.
And best of all, there were dozens and dozens
of delicious doughnuts!

For dessert, Detective Dog
always ordered a doughnut.
Detective Dog LOVED doughnuts.

"Hot diggity dog!" said the detective.
"It's a birthday party!"

Suddenly, the light flashed on.
"SURPRISE!" yelled Detective Dog's friends.

One day after dinner, Detective Dog said to Dave
"Today is my birthday. I think I will have
TWO doughnuts for dessert to celebrate."
"On the double, detective," said Dave.

The trail lead right into Debbie's Deli.
"The doughnut-napper must be in here!"
said Detective Dog.

Suddenly, Detective Dog noticed something
near the door. Powdered sugar!
"If I follow this trail of doughnut dust,
I bet I'll find the thief!" she said.

"Oh, dear!" Dave cried.
"The doughnuts have disappeared!"
"Doggone it!" said Detective Dog.
"I have some detecting to do!"

4

C

Detective Dog turned the doorknob.
She stepped inside the deli.
It was completely dark.

9

Detective Dog followed the trail
of doughnut dust downtown.

6

D

She followed it past Drake's Drugstore
and the department store.

7

Ee Cheer

E is for elephant, E is for ear

E is for elk, a kind of deer

E is for egg, elbow, and eye

E is for eagle that soars through the sky

Hooray for E, big and small—

the most excellent, exciting letter of all!

Ee

The Enormous Elephant Show

BY LIZA CHARLESWORTH

ILLUSTRATED BY NADINE BERNARD WESTCOTT

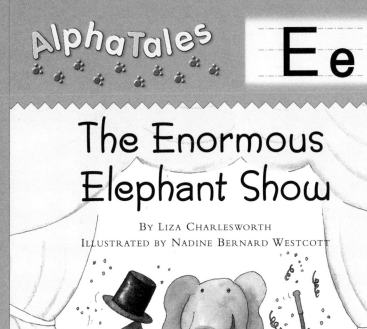

Elvin the Elephant exercises with a cow!

The Enormous Elephant Show Starring Elvin

Let me entertain you...

Elvin the Elephant is waiting backstage.
To start his show, just turn the page.

To my elegant niece, Madeleine —
of whom I'm ENORMOUSLY proud!

❀ ❀ ❀ ❀

A

Elvin the Elephant takes an enormous bow!

13

Elvin the Elephant makes an E out of eels!

Elvin the Elephant eats a mountain of peas!

2

B

11

Elvin the Elephant climbs evergreen trees!

Elvin the Elephant tosses eggplants to seals!

Elvin the Elephant models elegant clothes!

Elvin the Elephant bakes elderberry pies!

Elvin the Elephant does excellent dives!

Elvin the Elephant skates with eggs on his toes!

Elvin the Elephant pulls an elk from a hat!

Elvin the Elephant sends e-mail to his cat!

Ff Cheer

F is for ferret, **F** is for flute

F is for flower, feather, and fruit

F is for frog, friend, and French fries

F is for fox and fireflies

Hooray for **F** big and small—

the most fantastic, fabulous letter of all!

14

Fifi Ferret's Flute

By Samantha Berger
Illustrated by Anne Kennedy

1

Fifi was so happy to have her flute back!

12

When Fifi Ferret was five years old,
her father gave her a flute.

F is for Felicia, Fluppers, Frau,
Fred-n-Phran, & Ms. Fleming —
fabulous forever.

A

But Fifi was even happier to have
such fabulous friends.

Fifi Ferret loved her flute…

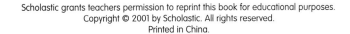

She played it for her
family.

She played it
in the forest.

She played it in fields
of flowers.

She grabbed the flute right before it fell
down the falls!

B

All of a sudden, Fish leapt from the water.

My flute!

One day, Fifi was playing her flute by the river. Suddenly, the flute fell from Fifi's hands!

The flute floated past Flamingo, who was fluffing her feathers. "Follow that flute!" yelled Fifi, Frog, Fawn, and Fox.

The flute floated past Frog, who was catching flies. "Follow that flute!" yelled Fifi.

The flute floated far, far away.
Fifi ran after it.

Fifi, Frog, Fawn, Fox, and Flamingo ran fast.
But the flute floated faster.
"Oh no! It's floating toward the falls!" Fifi cried.
Fifi feared her flute would be lost forever.

The flute floated past Fawn,
who was nibbling ferns.
"Follow that flute!" yelled Fifi and Frog.

The flute floated past Fox, who was eating figs.
"Follow that flute!" yelled Fifi, Frog, and Fawn.

Gg Cheer

G is for gorillas, on the loose

G is for gopher, goldfish, and goose

G is for granny, giggle, and glass

G is for gumdrops, grapes, and grass

Hooray for **G**, big and small—

the grandest, greatest letter of all!

Gorilla, Be Good!

BY MARIA FLEMING
ILLUSTRATED BY MATT PHILLIPS

On Monday, I went to visit Gorilla at the zoo.
Guess who followed me home?

On Monday, I went to the zoo.
Guess who followed me home?

For a great group of friends
(in alphabetical order):
Alex, Dave, Emma, Hannah, Ryan, and Trish.

A gorilla!
I asked my mom if he could stay.
"If he is a good guest," Mom said.

"He has been a terrible guest!"

"That gorilla must go!" Mom said.

On Tuesday, Gorilla broke Granny's glasses and gabbed on the phone all day.

On Sunday, Gorilla invited a gang of friends over. The gorillas played golf and other games.

On Thursday, Gorilla gobbled up a gooseberry pie, a gallon of ice cream, and other goodies.

On Wednesday, Gorilla trampled the grapes growing in the garden.

They made a great mess.

BOO!

On Friday, Gorilla dressed like a ghost and scared the goldfish.

On Saturday, Gorilla glued gumdrops to Dad's galoshes.

Hh Cheer

H is for honeybee, **H** is for hen

H is for hamster and hogs in a pen

H is for hiccups, hat, hug, and horse

H is for hula-hoop and hippo of course

Hooray for **H**, big and small—

the happiest, hoppiest letter of all!

14

Hide-and-Seek Hippo

BY SAMANTHA BERGER
ILLUSTRATED BY MAXIE CHAMBLISS

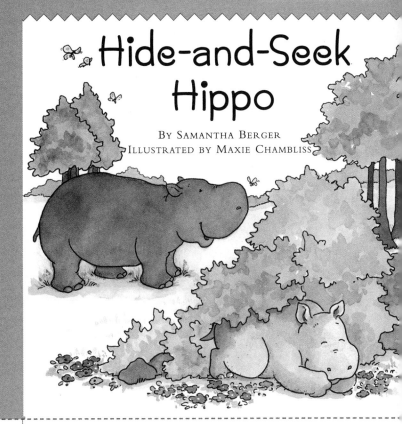

Where could Baby Hippo be hiding?
Mother Hippo has something for him...

12

Have you seen Baby Hippo?
It's time for him to come home.

1

A

...a great big hippo hug!

He must be here somewhere!

B

Is he hiding in the hyenas' hideaway?

Is he hiding in Hummingbird's honeysuckle?

Is he hiding in Horse's haystack?

Is he hiding in Hare's hutch?

Is he hiding in Hedgehog's hole?

Is he hiding behind the honeybees' hive?

Is he hiding in the hens' house?

Ii Cheer

I is for iguana and ice cream, too

I is for island in the ocean blue

I is for igloo and ivy patch

I is for icicle and an itch to scratch

Hooray for **I**, big and small—

the most incredible letter of all!

14

Iguana on Ice

BY CAROL PUGLIANO-MARTIN
ILLUSTRATED BY ELLEN JOY SASAKI

Iggy eats ice cream.

Iggy ice skates.

Iggy floats on icebergs.

Iggy licks icicles.

Iggy Iguana lives on an island.

12

1

To Scott, who also thinks that ice is nice.

A

And every night, Iggy sleeps
inside Izzy's igloo—
which is even better than an icebox!

13

Iggy's island is very hot.
The heat makes Iggy feel ill.

2

B

Now Iggy is in Iceland with Izzy.

11

The postcard gives Iggy an idea.
"I'll go to Iceland to visit Izzy!" says Iggy.

To stay cool, Iggy floats in his inner tube.

Iggy even imagines sitting in front of
an icebox with ice cubes!

Iggy imagines ice skating.

Iggy imagines icy things.
He imagines eating ice cream.

C

One day, Iggy gets a postcard
from his cousin Izzy in Iceland.

Iggy imagines floating on an iceberg.

D

Iggy imagines licking icicles.

Jj Cheer

J is for jaguars, jumping high

J is for jam, jeep, and July

J is for jungle, jug, jar, and jeans

J is for juice and jellybeans

Hooray for **J**, big and small—

the jazziest, jolliest letter of all!

Jj

Jaguar's Jungleberry Jamboree

BY HELEN H. MOORE

ILLUSTRATED BY ELLEN JOY SASAKI

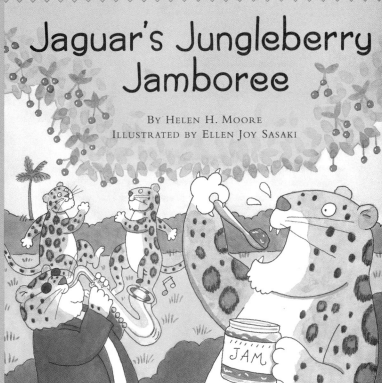

Jeremy joined the jamboree.
He jumped. He jitterbugged. He jived.
And he ate jungleberry jam until he thought
he would burst.

Jeremy Jaguar loved jam.
Jungleberry jam was Jeremy's favorite.

To my wonderful nephew,
the marvelous Max.

A

When the jamboree was over, Jeremy packed his jeep with jam jars and drove home.
Now every July, he joins the other jaguars for the jungleberry jamboree. And the jaguar who eats the most jam is always Jeremy!

13

Jeremy loved jam on toast

jam on pancakes

The jaguars were jumping,
jitterbugging, and jiving.
And best of all,
they were making jam!

2

B

11

"Jumping June bugs!" said Jeremy.
"It's a jaguar jamboree!"
Jaguars from every part of the jungle
had come to pick jungleberries.

jam on muffins

even jam on ham!

As Jeremy got closer to the jungleberry trees,
he heard jazzy music playing.

"I must pick some jungleberries
to make more jam," said Jeremy.
Jeremy waited until the first day of July,
when the jungleberries would be ripe.

One day, a terrible thing happened.
Jeremy Jaguar ran out of jam!

Jeremy peeked through the bushes.

Jeremy put on his jersey and jumped
in his jeep. He drove through the jungle
to the place where the jungleberry trees grew.

Soon he saw the trees up ahead.
The jungleberries were as bright as jewels!

Kk Cheer

K is for king and kangaroo

K is for kettle, key, and kazoo

K is for koala, **K** is for kite

K is for a kiss goodnight

Hooray for **K**, big and small—

the kookiest, kickiest letter of all!

Kangaroo Kazoo

By Wendy Cheyette Lewison
Illustrated by Rusty Fletcher

So long!
Thanks for coming!

Red or yellow, green or orange,
purple, pink, or blue–

This kangaroo has a red kazoo.
She takes it everywhere.

A

you can have all kinds of fun
with a kangaroo kazoo!

13

This kangaroo has a pink kazoo.
He plays it at the fair.

2

B

Then the king's kooky kin
all kick up their heels.
They do the kazooky-pooky
and the kazarama reel.

11

They play all day,
they never stop,
while the kangaroo king
does the kangaroo hop.

This kangaroo has a yellow kazoo.
She plays it in the spring.

...to join the best band in the land

This kangaroo has a blue kazoo
to play on the deep blue sea.

This kangaroo has a green kazoo.
It makes the katydids sing.

and play at the kangaroo dance.

This kangaroo has a purple kazoo
from the purple kazooka tree.

This kangaroo has an orange kazoo,
and now he has a chance...

Ll Cheer

L is for lamb and licorice stick

L is for lots of lollipops to lick

L is for lion and ladybug

L is for leaf and lemonade in a jug

Hooray for **L**, big and small—

the loveliest, luckiest letter of all!

14

The Lamb Who Loved to Laugh

By Carol Pugliano-Martin
Illustrated by Hans Wilhelm

Lulu still likes to laughs at her friends …

12

Lulu the Lamb loved to laugh.

1

To Baxter, a lad who loves to laugh.

A

but only when they tell her a funny joke!

Lulu laughed at Ladybug
because she was so little.

B

"From now on, I will laugh less,"
Lulu promised her friends.
"At last, Lulu has learned her lesson!"
said Ladybug.

Ladybug, Llama, Lizard, Leopard, and Lion laughed at Lulu.
Lulu didn't like being laughed at one little bit!

Lulu laughed at Llama when he spilled pink lemonade at lunch.

Lulu laughed at Lion.
She laughed and laughed and laughed.

Lulu laughed at Leopard's lavender leotard.

Lulu laughed at Lizard
when she fell off the ladder.

C

Lion looked angry. He roared at Lulu.
Lion roared so loud, he made Lulu fall…
right into the lake!

The other animals did not like Lulu's laughing.
It made them feel low.
"Someday, Lulu will learn," said Leopard.

D

Lulu walked along, laughing loudly.
She bumped into Lion, who was licking a lollipop.
The lollipop got stuck in Lion's mane!

Mm Cheer

M is for monkey, marbles, and mop

M is for mitten and mountaintop

M is for mouse and the moon in the sky

M is for muffin, milk, and mud pie

Hooray for **M**, big and small—

the most magical, marvelous letter of all!

Monkey's Miserable Monday

BY VALERIE GARFIELD
ILLUSTRATED BY JAMES YOUNG

Monkey's mother makes him a mug of cocoa
with mini marshmallows.
Then she mixes up a batch of maple muffins—
Monkey's favorite!

Monkey is in a bad mood.
He woke up late and now he must hurry
or he'll miss the school bus.
"This Monday morning is off to a miserable start!"
Monkey mutters.

For MSG & DLG,
who endured mean Mondays
with three monkeys.

A

Monkey spends the rest of the morning drawing meadows and mountains with his magic markers. "What a MARVELOUS Sunday," says Monkey. And it is.

13

The bus will be here in a few minutes, but Monkey can't find any socks that match. "What a miserable Monday!" Monkey mutters.

B

"Now I'm going to miss the bus!" Monkey moans. "What a miserable Monday!" Monkey's mother gives him a hug and smiles.
"But munchkin, today isn't Monday," she says. "It's only Sunday!"

11

Monkey tells his mother about the socks that don't match, the spilled milk, the mustard sandwich, the mistakes on his math homework, the lost mittens, the mat, and the marbles.

At breakfast, Monkey spills the milk. "What a miserable Monday!" Monkey mutters as he mops up the mess.

All of his marbles roll out of his bag. Monkey is mad. "I hate Mondays!" Monkey moans.

It is snowing outside. Monkey can't find his mittens anywhere. "What a miserable Monday!" Monkey mutters.

Monkey has misplaced his lunch money,
so he must make a sandwich.
But there is no lunch meat, only mustard.
"What a miserable Monday!" Monkey mutters.

Monkey's mother comes to the door.
"What's the matter, my little monkey?" she asks.

Monkey looks over his math homework.
He sees two mistakes!
"What a miserable Monday!" Monkey mutters.

Monkey runs out the door to catch the bus.
Whoops! He trips on the mat.

Nn Cheer

N is for newt, noodle, and nose

N is for needle to sew torn clothes

N is for newspaper, nut, nail, and nest

N is for nap, when you need to rest

Hooray for **N**, big and small—

the niftiest, neatest letter of all!

The Nicest Newt

BY HEATHER FELDMAN
ILLUSTRATED BY PAUL HARVEY

Sometimes, even nice newts are naughty.

Nate, you are the nicest newt!

Nate is a very nice newt.

For Mark and Sophie.

A

13

Nate brings his father
the newspaper.

B

Nate nibbles and nibbles on the cake.
Soon, there is none left.

Being nice can make a Newt hungry.
Nate needs a snack.
He sees a cake that Nana Newt
has made for dessert.

Nate helps his neighbors.

Nate always keeps his room neat.

At noon, Nate neatly folds the napkins
for lunch.

Nate is never noisy when his mother is working.

Nate loans his friend Natalie a nickel so she can buy a new necklace.

After lunch, Nate tucks his nine brothers in for naps.

Nate helps his sister learn her numbers.

Oo Cheer

O is for octopus who lives in the sea

O is for owl, high in a tree

O is overalls and oars for a boat

O is for ostrich, orange, and oat

Hooray for O, big and small—

the most outstanding letter of all!

Oo

Olive the Octopus's Day of Juggling

By Liza Charlesworth
Illustrated by Matt Phillips

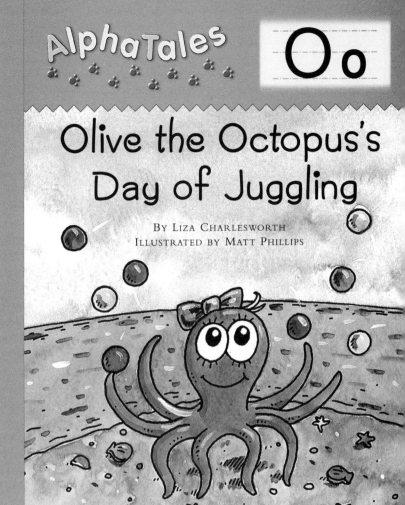

OUCH!

OLIVE

Olive is an octopus.
She lives in the ocean.

To the OH-so-fabulous Gerald K.,
who's great at keeping lots
of balls in the air!

A

Now, Olive dreams of becoming an organist.
She practices around the clock.

13

Olive dreams of becoming a juggler.
She practices around the clock.

B

and the owl in the oak tree and the orangutan
and the orange alien from outer space
and even the entire orchestra—
right on Olive's head!

11

At seven o'clock, Olive gets
oh so sleepy and...OOOPS!
Down come the onion
and the old pair of overalls

At one o'clock, Olive juggles an onion.

At six o'clock, Olive adds an entire orchestra.

At three o'clock, Olive adds an owl
in an oak tree.

At two o'clock, Olive juggles an onion and an old pair of overalls.

At four o'clock, Olive adds an orangutan.

At five o'clock, Olive adds an orange alien from outer space.

Pp Cheer

P is for pig, pickles, and pot

P is for pizza, gooey and hot

P is for pancakes, piled up high

P is for puppy, popcorn, and pie

Hooray for **P**, big and small—

the peachiest, peppiest letter of all!

14

The Pigs' Picnic

By Helen H. Moore
Illustrated by Ellen Joy Sasaki

Pizza!

And they did!

12

Penny, Polly, and Peter Pig were planning a picnic.
"What shall we pack in our picnic basket?"
asked Penny.

1

To the precious, petite princess, Rachel Collins.

A

13

Peter looked in the pantry.
"Let's pack some peaches," said Peter.
"A peachy idea!" said Polly.
"Are they ripe?" asked Penny.
"Perhaps we should taste them first," said Polly.

"That's peculiar!" said Peter.
"I guess we'll have to put off our picnic," said Polly.
"We could order pizza instead," said Penny.

2

B

11

Before long, the pantry was empty.
But so was the picnic basket!
Penny, Polly, and Peter were puzzled.

And they did.
"Perfect!" said Penny.

"Perhaps we should pack some pasta salad,"
said Polly.
"And pears and plums," said Penny.

And they did.
"MMMMMMM. Pickle-icious!" said Peter.

"Let's pack pickles," said Peter.
"Perhaps we should taste the pickles, too,"
said Polly.

"And pumpkin pie," said Peter.
Of course, Penny, Polly, and Peter
tasted everything first.

Peter made some peanut butter
and potato chip sandwiches.
"Would you like to taste them?"
Peter asked Penny and Polly.

"Yes, please!" said Penny and Polly.
And they did.

Qq Cheer

Q is for quail and a quilt for your bed

Q is for queen, with a crown on her head

Q is for quack and a quarter to spend

Q is for a quarrel you have with a friend

Hooray for **Q**, big and small—

the quaintest, quirkiest letter of all!

The Quiet Quail

BY HEATHER FELDMAN

ILLUSTRATED BY RUSTY FLETCHER

Queenie is quick, but the other animals are quicker. They snatch Quincy's quilt from Queenie's teeth. They give the quilt back to Quincy.

Quincy is a quiet quail.
He likes to do quiet things.
Quincy likes to snuggle with his favorite quilt and listen to the quiet pitter-pat of the rain.

For Ryan, Brittany, Jody, and Doug.

Quincy thanks all the animals for rescuing her quilt, especially Dottie.
"Your loud quacking saved the day!" Quincy tells Dottie. And for once, the quiet quail is happy to have such a noisy friend.

Quincy likes to sit quietly and read.

The other animals hear Dottie's loud quacking. They chase Queenie.

Queenie runs right past Dottie.
"THAT'S QUINCY'S QUILT!" quacks Dottie.
"CATCH QUEENIE! QUICK!"

Quincy likes to take quiet walks.

Quincy decides to go for a swim to drown
out Dottie's quacking. He spreads his quilt
on the grass and jumps in the pond.

"QUACK! QUACK! QUACK! HI, QUINCY!
QUACK, QUACK!" shouts Dottie.
"Hello, Dottie," whispers the quiet quail.

Sometimes on his quiet walks,
Quincy meets his friend Dottie Duck.
Dottie is not very quiet.
In fact, Dottie is quite loud.

C

Suddenly, Queenie the dog trots by.
She grabs Quincy's quilt and runs away.
"My quilt!" cries Quincy. "Someone stop
Queenie!" But Quincy's voice is too quiet.
No one hears him.

Quincy and Dottie sit in the park.
"QUACK! QUACK! QUACK! QUACK! QUACK!"
shouts Dottie. "WHAT A BEAUTIFUL DAY!
QUACK! QUACK!"

D

Dottie quacks and quacks till Quincy's head hurts.
"Dottie, please quit quacking," says Quincy.
But Dottie is quacking so loudly, she does not
hear the quiet quail.

Rr Cheer

R is for rabbit, radish, and rose

R is for ribbon and the rooster that crows

R is for run, rope, rock, and red

R is for raindrops that fall on your head

Hooray for **R**, big and small—

the most remarkable letter of all!

14

Rosie Rabbit's Radish

By Wendy Cheyette Lewison
Illustrated by Rusty Fletcher

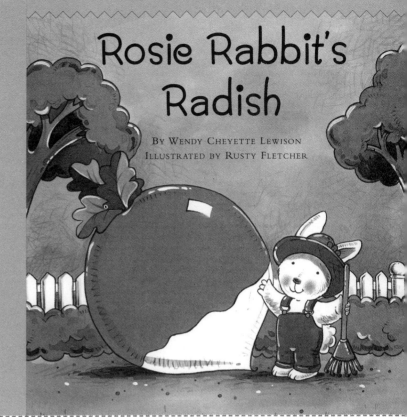

She will take it to the fair…

Rosie Rabbit has a radish.

A

Rah, Rah, Rosie!

and win a blue ribbon!

Rosie takes good care of her radish.
She rakes the ground around it.
She removes rocks.

B

What will Rosie do with her radish?

Rick and Rita help Rosie roll the radish down the road.

Rosie rakes and rakes—even in the rain! She does not rest.

Rosie ties a rope around the radish.
Rick and Rita help her pull up the radish root.

But Rosie would rather take care of her radish.

"Come for a ride," says Rick Rooster.
"Let's roller-skate," says Rita Raccoon.

What a rare radish!
It is red and round and really big!

At night, Rosie sits in her rocking chair.
She reads to her radish and plays the radio.

The radish grows and grows.
Soon the radish is ripe.
It is ready to be picked.

Ss Cheer

S is for spider, snake, snail, and seal

S is for a super-sized sandwich meal

S is for sailboat, smile, and sing

S is for spaghetti, seesaw, and swing

Hooray for **S**, big and small—

the most sensational letter of all!

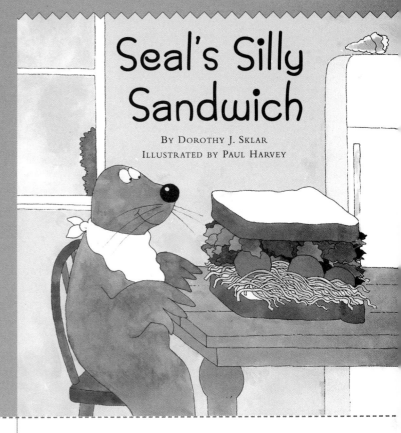

Seal's Silly Sandwich

By Dorothy J. Sklar
Illustrated by Paul Harvey

But Seal didn't think his sandwich was silly at all.

One Sunday, Seal invited his friends for supper.

A

He thought it was scrumptious!

"What's for supper?" said Snail.
"I am serving a sandwich," said Seal.

B

"No thanks," said Snail, Sloth, Snake,
Salamander, Skunk, Spider, and Squirrel.
"That sandwich is just too silly!"

"Who's ready for a slice of my sandwich?"
said Seal.

Seal put some sardines on a slice of bread.
"Sardines in a sandwich!" said Snail.
"That's silly!"

Next Seal added six scoops
of strawberry ice cream.
"Strawberry ice cream in a sandwich!"
said Spider. "That's silly!"

Next Seal added some spaghetti.
"Spaghetti in a sandwich!" said Snake.
"That's silly!"

Next Seal added some stew.
"Stew in a sandwich!" said Sloth.
"That's silly!"

Next Seal added some salsa and some maple syrup.
"Salsa and syrup in a sandwich!" said Squirrel.
"That's silly!"

Next Seal added some spinach.
"Spinach in a sandwich!" said Salamander.
"That's silly!"

Next Seal added some scrambled eggs.
"Scrambled eggs in a sandwich!" said Skunk.
"That's silly!"

Tt Cheer

T is for turtle, tiger, and toad

T is for taxi driving down the road

T is for table and telephone booth

T is for teacup, tickle, and tooth

Hooray for T, big and small—

the most totally terrific letter of all!

14

When Tilly Turtle Came to Tea

BY CAROL PUGLIANO-MARTIN
ILLUSTRATED BY RUSTY FLETCHER

When Tilly Turtle came to tea,
She saved the party cheerfully.

12

When Tilly Turtle came to tea,
She took a taxi to the tree,
Where the party was to be,
When Tilly Turtle came to tea.

1

To Zach, who also has a useful back.

A

She turned into a table—see?
When Tilly Turtle came to tea.

13

When Tilly Turtle came to tea,
She arrived on time at three,

2

B

When Tilly Turtle came to tea,
She said, "If you will both agree,
Please put the tablecloth on me!"
When Tilly Turtle came to tea.

11

When Tilly Turtle came to tea,
She told her friends, "Please pardon me,
For the topsy-turvy mess you see!"
When Tilly Turtle came to tea.

Looking pretty as could be,
When Tilly Turtle came to tea.

When Tilly Turtle came to tea,
The teacups tumbled, oh dear me!

And toast and tarts beneath the tree,
When Tilly Turtle came to tea.

When Tilly Turtle came to tea,
There were tiny teacups set for three,

What a terrible sight to see!
When Tilly Turtle came to tea.

When Tilly Turtle came to tea,
Her friends Tiger and Toad and she,
Told tall tales and laughed with glee,
When Tilly Turtle came to tea.

When Tilly Turtle came to tea,
She laughed so hard she could not see,
And tipped the table with her knee,
When Tilly Turtle came to tea.

Uu Cheer

U is for umbrellabird and an umbrella
to share

U is for unicycle and underwear

U is for unicorn, umpire, and us

U is for uncle and uptown bus

Hooray for **U**, big and small—

the most unbelievable letter of all!

Umbrellabird's Umbrella

BY HEATHER FELDMAN
ILLUSTRATED BY NADINE BERNARD WESTCOTT

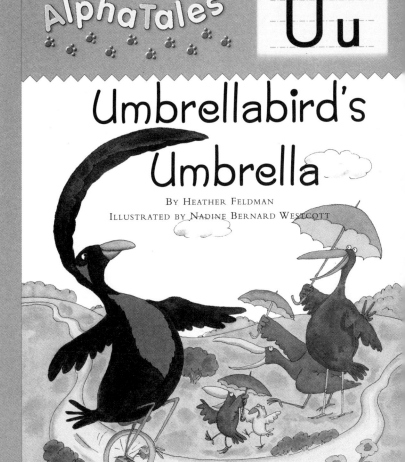

Now Umbrellabird holds his head up
high when he is out riding his unicycle.

Umbrellabird is unlike any other bird.
He has very unusual feathers.

For Joshua and Jeremy.

And sometimes, Umbrellabird even wishes
for a little rain!

The other birds tease Umbrellabird about his
unusual feathers. They think his feathers
look like a giant umbrella.

All the birds thank Umbrellabird.
"Your wonderful umbrella kept us dry," they say.
"We are sorry we upset you with our teasing.
We wish we had umbrellas like you!"

"Quickly! Quickly!" says Umbrellabird
as the other birds duck under his feathers.
The birds stay under Umbrellabird's umbrella
until the rain stops.

"Why is your umbrella up?"
the other birds ask Umbrellabird.
"Is it going to rain today?"

Suddenly, it begins to pour.
But Umbrellabird notices that he
is not getting wet. Umbrellabird's umbrella
is keeping him dry!

One day, Umbrellabird decides to visit his uncle.
He hops on his unicycle and peddles uptown.

The teasing makes Umbrellabird very unhappy.
He tries to hide his feathers under a hat.
But it is no use. His umbrella always pops up.

The other birds look for a dry place.
Umbrellabird calls to them.
"Come under my umbrella.
It's dry under here!"

"Look at those ugly feathers!"
the other birds call as Umbrellabird rides by.
Umbrellabird pretends not to hear them.

He looks up at the sky
and keeps on pedaling.
"Uh-oh!" says Umbrellabird.
He sees dark clouds, way up high.

Vv Cheer

V is for viper and valentine, too

V is for delicious vegetable stew

V is for violin, village, and vase

V is for van and vacation days

Hooray for **V**, big and small—

the very, VERY best letter of all!

Vera Viper's Valentine

By Maxwell Higgins

Illustrated by James Young

On the way home, Vera and Victor stopped for vanilla ice cream cones in the village.

Vera Viper and Victor Viper were best friends. Every Sunday, Vera would visit Victor.

And that Sunday, Vera was the happiest viper in the whole world!

A

13

Vera and Victor would play volleyball...

Then Vera and Victor played volleyball.

They watched videos.

They drove through the valley.

B

11

Victor read Vera the verse on the valentine.
"Thank you, Victor," said Vera.
"I am very glad you are my best friend, too!"

...and watch videos.

The next Sunday, Vera stayed home.
She watched videos, but it wasn't
any fun without Victor.
Then there was a knock at Vera's door.

Vera and Victor liked to stop in the village
for vanilla ice cream cones.

Sometimes they would go for a drive
through the valley.

C

It was Victor! Victor handed Vera a big red valentine.
"I'm sorry I haven't been able to visit," said Victor.
"I have been busy making you this valentine."

One Sunday, Vera Viper knocked on Victor's door.
"Vera, I cannot visit with you today," said Victor.
"I am very, very busy."

D

The next Sunday, Victor was still busy.
And the Sunday after that, too.
Vera Viper was very, very sad.
"I don't think Victor wants
to be friends anymore," Vera said.

Ww Cheer

W is for worm and a wagon to pull
W is for wig, whale, wave, and wool
W is for watermelon, juicy and sweet
W is for walnuts, waffles, and wheat
Hooray for **W**, big and small—
the wildest, wackiest letter of all!

Worm's Wagon

BY SAMANTHA BERGER
ILLUSTRATED BY MATT PHILLIPS

When the wagon was fixed,
Worm wiggled into it.

One day, Worm went to the woods
to gather walnuts.
He brought his wagon with him.

W is for the wonderful and wise Arianne Weber.
With warmest wishes.

A

Then Wombat, Weasel, Wolf, Woodpecker,
Walrus, and Whale pulled Worm all the way home
And weary Worm had a wonderful ride.

13

On his way home, Worm saw Woodpecker
whistling in a weeping willow.
Woodpecker asked Worm for a ride.

2

B

Worm's friends worked on the wagon all afternoon.

11

"Don't worry, Worm," the animals said.

Worm wiggled along, pulling Woodpecker in his wagon. Soon they came upon Weasel eating watermelon.
Weasel asked Worm for a ride.

Worm wiggled with all his might trying to pull Woodpecker, Weasel, Wombat, Wolf, Walrus, and Whale in the wagon. But the wagon would not move. The wheels started to wobble.

Worm wiggled along, pulling Woodpecker, Weasel, and Wombat in his wagon.
Next, they met Wolf on his way to work.
Wolf asked Worm for a ride.

Worm wiggled along, pulling Woodpecker and Weasel in his wagon. Before long, they bumped into Wombat wearing her new wig. Wombat asked Worm for a ride.

WHAM!
The weight was too much for the wagon.
It crashed to the ground.
"Oh, no! My wagon!" Worm wailed.

Worm wiggled along, pulling Woodpecker, Weasel, Wombat, and Wolf in his wagon. Soon they saw Walrus winking and waving. Walrus asked Worm for a ride.

Worm wiggled along, pulling Woodpecker, Weasel, Wombat, Wolf, and Walrus in his wagon. Up ahead, they saw Whale playing in the water. Whale asked Worm for a ride.

Xx Cheer

X is for x-ray fish, swimming along

X is for xylophone, to play a song

What else starts with **X**? Not a whole lot.

But in tic-tac-toe, **X** marks the spot.

Hooray for **X**, big and small—

the most exceptional letter of all!

A Xylophone for X-Ray Fish

BY LIZA CHARLESWORTH
ILLUSTRATED BY JAMES YOUNG

X-ray Fish plays "Happy Birthday"
on his new xylophone.
All his friends sing extra loud.

Today, X-ray Fish feels extra special.
It is his birthday!
X-ray Fish is expecting friends for a party.

To my eXcellent mom, Sylvia Charlesworth—
XOXOXOXOXOXOXOXOXOXOXOXOXOXOXOXOXOX!

A

Then it is time to eat cake.
X-ray Fish is excited. With his x-ray vision,
he can see it is his favorite kind—
chocolate with seaweed filling!

13

The party is extremely fun.
Everyone plays pin-the-tail-on-the-seahorse
and other exciting games.

2

B

It is a xylophone!
"Thank you for the excellent gift," says X-ray Fish.
Then he unwraps it. "It is exactly what I wanted!"

11

There is one present left to open. The tag says,
"To X-ray Fish from Mom. XOXOXOXO."
"All those X's mean I love you,"
his mom explains.
Will this present be a xylophone?

At last, it is time for X-ray Fish to open his gifts.
He knows exactly what he wants—a xylophone!

Then Tigerfish gives X-ray Fish a present.
Is it a xylophone?

No, but it is an excellent gift!
"Thanks for the ball!" exclaims X-ray Fish.

X-ray Fish has x-ray vision.
He uses it to examine each gift before
he opens it. Angelfish gives X-ray Fish a present.
Is it a xylophone?

No, but it is an excellent gift!
"Thanks for the teddy bear,"
exclaims X-ray Fish.

Next, Blowfish gives X-ray Fish a present.
Is it a xylophone?

No, but it is an excellent gift!
"Thanks for the boat!" exclaims X-ray Fish.

Yy Cheer

Y is for yo-yo, **Y** is for yak

Y is for a yummy yogurt snack

Y is for yarn, yes, yard, and young

Y is for yam and a bright yellow sun

Hooray for big **Y**, small **y**, too—

the letter that makes you want to yell

     "YAHOO!"

The Yak Who Yelled Yuck

BY CAROL PUGLIANO-MARTIN
ILLUSTRATED BY PAUL HARVEY

She tasted the yellow banana,
the yogurt, and the yam.
"YOWEEE!" said the young yak.
"These are yummy!"

There once was a young yak
who hated trying new foods.

To Sophie, who never yells "Yuck."

A

And now she's the yak who yells, "YUM!"

13

One day, the young yak's father gave her a yellow banana.

2

B

The young yak leaped over the fence into her neighbor's yard.

11

"YOO-HOO, young yak!"
the wise old yak yelled over the fence.
"Yes?" said the young yak.
"You should taste things before you yell yuck,"
said the wise old yak.

"YUCK!" yelled the yak without
even taking a bite.
The yak tossed the yellow banana
into her neighbor's yard.

A wise old yak lived next door to the young yak.
He was in his yard playing with his yo-yo.

"YUCK!" yelled the yak.
She tossed the yogurt into her neighbor's yard.

The young yak's father
gave her some yogurt.

4

The yam hit the wise old yak right in the head!
"YIKES!" yelled the wise old yak.

9

The young yak's father gave her a yam.

6

"YUCK!" yelled the yak.
She tossed the yam into her neighbor's yard.

7

Zz Cheer

Z is for zebra, **Z** is for zoo

Z is for zucchini and ziti, too

Z is for zipper, **Z** is for zap

Z is for zzzzzzz when you nap

Hooray for **Z**, big and small—

the zippiest, zaniest letter of all!

14

Zack the Lazy Zebra

BY WENDY CHEYETTE LEWISON
ILLUSTRATED BY CLIVE SCRUTON

No!
Now two zebras
want to sleep!

Zz-zz-zz
Zz-zz-zz

12

Zack the Zebra lives at the zoo.
All day long, what does Zack do?

1

A

At last, the zookeepers
give up their schemes.
They wish Zack and Zed
sweet zebra dreams.
Zz-zz-zz
Zz-zz-zz

13

Zz-zz-zz

2

B

Will Zed make Zack
wake up and leap?

11

He zooms and zigzags
around everything.

The zookeepers bring a zebra snack.
But it doesn't wake up Zack.
Zack has no zest.
He wants to rest.

Zz-zz-zz

Zack thinks their tricks are boring.
He goes on snoring.

Zz-zz-zz

They bang a drum.
They tickle his nose.

Zack's eyes stay closed.
He wants to doze.

Zz-zz-zz

They zap Zack with
a garden hose.

Look! Here comes Zed,
a zebra with zing!

They try a zillion zany tricks.

They hop around on pogo sticks.

Notes

Notes

Notes

Notes